BABYLON

A History From Beginning to End

Table of Contents

battle the world had ever seen at that time, Sargon took over all the Sumerian city-states and incorporated them into the growing Akkadian Empire.

Hungry for more, Sargon sent his armies into the lands ruled by the Assyrians to the north and the Elamites to the east. He defeated them both, and by the time that Sargon died in around 2279 BCE, the Akkadian Empire was the largest in the world. Before his death, Sargon established a port city on the Euphrates River. This was Babylon, a small town distributed equally on the left and right banks of the mighty river, around sixty miles south of modern-day Baghdad.

The lack of reliable records from this period makes it difficult to be certain precisely when the city was founded. Several dates are mentioned in ancient texts. The Greek writer Stephen of Byzantium claimed that Babylon was founded 1,002 years before the siege of Troy, in 2231 BCE. Roman historian Pliny the Elder believed that astronomical observations were first undertaken in Babylon 490 years before the Greek era of Phoroneus, in 2243 BCE. Another Greek historian, Diodorus Siculus, who claimed to have access to ancient Babylonian writings, believed that the city was founded in 2286 BCE. Most likely, the city first emerged in the twenty-third century BCE, around the time when Sargon of Akkad was building his mighty Akkadian Empire.

Some scholars claim that the name of the city is Sumerian in origin and means "God's gate." Most accounts seem to agree that the city was first ruled by a king named Belus. In its early days, Babylon grew from being a small port town into becoming one of the more prosperous cities in Mesopotamia, though it was overshadowed by the many larger city-states in the area including Larsa, Ur, and Uruk, and it was closely associated with the nearby and more powerful city of Kazallu.

However, even as Babylon was growing, the Akkadian Empire was gradually being pushed back by the Amorites, tribes of semi-nomadic Hamitic-speaking people from Syria who, from the twenty-first century BCE, occupied large areas of southern Mesopotamia when they were forced out of their homeland by a severe and protracted drought. Sensibly, the Amorites did not face the powerful Akkadians in open battle—instead they seem to have infiltrated Akkadian cities gradually until they were strong enough to install their own leaders and dynasties. Over a period of around two hundred years, Akkadian cities in southern Mesopotamia came under Amorite control as Amorite grain merchants became wealthy and powerful citizens. These included several cities on the banks of the Euphrates such as Larsa, Lagash, and Babylon.

During the nineteenth century BCE, Babylon gained its first Amorite ruler, a local chief called Sumu-Abum. He did not claim to be king of Babylon and ruled the city as an *ensi*, a role roughly equivalent to a modern mayor, suggesting that the city was still of little importance. Nonetheless, Sumu-Abum is now considered to be the first king of the First Dynasty of Babylon (also known as the Amorite Dynasty). His successor, Sumu-la-El, is credited with completing the building of the first city walls and of achieving independence for Babylon from the city-state of Kazallu.

Babylon clearly prospered under Amorite rule, though it remained a relatively small city which exercised control of only a very limited area. Older and more powerful city-states in the area, including Elam, Isin, and Larsa, were much more significant at this time.

The fifth Amorite ruler of Babylon, Sin-Muballit, inherited the rule of the city from his father, Apil-Sin. Under the rule of Sin-Muballit, the city became more powerful, defeating an invading army from the larger city-state of Ur and then conquering the nearby city of Isin. Sin-Muballit improved the fortified walls of the city and declared himself king rather than ensi, reinforcing the notion that Babylon was now a fully independent city-state.

We know relatively little about the foundation of Babylon (and even most of the facts quoted here have been disputed by some historians) partly because the water table in the area where Babylon was built has risen considerably in the intervening years meaning that the remains of the early city have vanished or are underwater and not accessible to archeologists. Most of what we know comes from records kept by the Sumerians and Akkadians, who both used cuneiform tablets, pieces of clay on to which writing was incised. Sumerian cuneiform tablets dating from the Third Dynasty of Ur have been discovered which provide tax records for the city of Babylon. However, very few artifacts have been found, and we know almost nothing about what life was like for inhabitants of the early city.

It wasn't until the sixth king of the First Babylonian Dynasty came to the throne that the city would suddenly grow in importance and power.

Chapter Two

King Hammurabi and the Babylonian Empire

"If a man put out the eye of another man, his eye shall be put out."

—The Hammurabi Code

Circa 1792 BCE, a new king took the throne in Babylon. Hammurabi was only around twenty years old when he became the sixth Amorite ruler of Babylon and the second to call himself king. King Sin-Muballit had suffered from continuing ill-health and had become too frail to rule when he abdicated in favor of his son.

When Hammurabi took the throne, the political situation in Mesopotamia was extremely complex and volatile. The network of city-states, all competing for control of the fertile lands between the Euphrates and Tigris Rivers, had coalesced into several large power blocks. The kingdom based in the city-state of Larsa controlled the vital Tigris River delta area. The upper reaches of the same river were controlled by the kingdom of Eshnunna. To the east lay the even more powerful kingdom of Elam which regularly sent armies into Mesopotamia to establish control over and demand tribute from the small, unaligned city-states in the area. In the north was the even larger kingdom of Assyria, ruled by the aggressive King Shamshi-Adad I who had already conquered lands and cities in Mesopotamia. Small city-states were regularly swallowed up by these larger kingdoms, and in the early years of his rule, Hammurabi was very careful not to offend any of his more powerful neighbors.

Instead, the young king concentrated on building and expanding temples within the city of Babylon and extending and improving the city's defensive walls. He also improved the defenses in the three other cities which were under the control of Babylon: Kish, Sippar, and Borsippa. Written records which survive suggest that King Hammurabi was a very able administrator as well as a hands-on ruler, personally overseeing a number of construction projects in the cities under his control.

Hammurabi also introduced a set of laws to be used in all the cities under his control, one of the earliest and most complete sets of laws developed by any human society. These laws, 282 in total, were carved using cuneiform text into a huge block of black diorite stone which was placed in the center of Babylon. The laws, which became known as the Hammurabi Code, are not a complete set of laws as we understand them today but rather a set of enactments which cover specific circumstances. They specify compensation for specific acts, for example: "If a man strike a free-born woman so that she lose her unborn child, he shall pay ten shekels for her loss," and, "If a man put out the eye of another man, his eye shall be put out."

The Hammurabi Code also covered commercial transactions: "If a physician heal the broken bone or diseased soft part of a man, the patient shall pay the physician five shekels in money," and, "If a veterinary surgeon perform a serious operation on an ass or an ox, and cure it, the owner shall pay the surgeon one-sixth of a shekel as a fee."

In addition, the Hammurabi Code provided guidance on actions expected of citizens in specific circumstances: "If anyone owe a debt for a loan, and a storm prostrates the grain, or the harvest fail, or the grain does not grow for lack of water; in that year he need not give his creditor any grain, he washes his debt-tablet in water and pays no rent for this year," and, "If he give a cultivated corn-field or a cultivated sesame-field, the corn or sesame in the field shall belong to the owner of the field, and he shall return the money to the merchant as rent."

The Hammurabi Code was one of the earliest attempts to enact a uniform set of behaviors which were expected to be adopted by all people in the kingdom, rich or poor. The intention was to foster a sense of fairness and equality amongst those ruled by King Hammurabi, and copies of the laws were distributed to all the cities under his control. This system might seem quite normal to us now, but in eighteenth-century BCE Mesopotamia, it was a revolutionary idea which directly influenced the laws of many succeeding civilizations. For example, in recognition of his creation of laws, King Hammurabi is shown on bas-relief carvings in the chamber of the United States House of Representatives in the Capitol Building in Washington, D.C.

For the first two decades of his reign, King Hammurabi managed to keep Babylon out of any major wars, and it seems likely that he might have continued to rule peacefully had not the kingdom of Elam initiated a plot designed to draw Babylon into conflict with the neighboring state of Larsa. The city-state of Elam had invaded and conquered the neighboring kingdom of Eshnunna. Then the Elamites developed a plot intended to make Hammurabi believe that Larsa was planning an attack. The plan of the Elamites was simple—they intended to sit back and watch while Larsa and Babylon fought each other and then attack the victor which would presumably be weakened after the war.

Hammurabi, however, didn't fall for the plot and instead he offered an alliance to Rim-Sin, the king of Larsa, in order to combine against Elam. Rim-Sin agreed, and Babylon and Larsa went to war with Elam. Up to this point, Hammurabi had not been involved in any wars, but he quickly proved to be as adept as a military leader as he was an administrator. The army of Babylon moved against the Elamites and utterly defeated them in a series of battles. Despite his success, Hammurabi was not happy with the performance of his allies from Larsa during the war with Elam. Almost all the fighting had been done by troops from Babylon, and Hammurabi came to believe that King Rim-Sin of Larsa was planning to wait until Babylon was weakened by the war with Elam to launch a sneak attack. To forestall this, Hammurabi turned on his ally, quickly taking the Larsa-controlled cities of Uruk, Isin, Nippur, and Lagash. This left the city of Larsa surrounded and cut off, and Rim-Sin surrendered soon after. In a startlingly short space of time, Hammurabi had proved himself to be an able military leader, and Babylon had suddenly become one of the most powerful states in Mesopotamia.

These short and successful wars seemed to have given Hammurabi a taste for conquest. In 1761 BCE, he suddenly broke off an alliance with King Zimri-Lim, ruler of the important and independent city of Mari. Mari was located on the upper reaches of the Euphrates River and was one of the wealthiest and most powerful cities in the area. In a short war, Hammurabi not only defeated the armies of Mari, but he also conquered the city and had it completely destroyed. This was uncharacteristic, and historians have wondered whether Hammurabi already had plans at this time to make Babylon the most influential city in Mesopotamia and wanted to remove Mari as a potential future rival. The conquest of Mari certainly gave Babylon complete control of the Euphrates River and notably increased its sphere of influence.

At this time, Hammurabi's forces also conquered one of the last remaining city-states in the area, Eshnunna. The city itself was too well defended to allow a successful attack, so Hammurabi instead dammed up the river which supplied the city with water and waited as the inhabitants began to die of thirst. It didn't take long for Eshnunna to surrender, and Hammurabi next turned his attention to the Assyrian Empire in the north. After a series of battles, the Assyrians were eventually beaten, and Hammurabi added many formerly Assyrian lands to those he already controlled.

By 1755 BCE, Hammurabi and Babylon controlled almost all of ancient Mesopotamia, and Hammurabi dubbed himself "King of the Four Quarters of the World" and named his kingdom Babylonia.

During the reign of Hammurabi, Babylon became the most important and most powerful city in the region. The city population grew to around 200,000, making it the largest city in the world at that time, and Babylon became the main trade hub of Mesopotamia. It also became a cultural and religious center. Hammurabi encouraged the pursuit of art, science, music, mathematics, literature, and astronomy, and the center of the city was dominated by a mighty ziggurat, a stepped pyramid, which was over three hundred feet tall and dominated a temple complex which covered many acres. The city itself included many gardens and wide, tree-lined streets as well as canals and was regarded as not just the largest but also the most beautiful city in the world.

The people of Babylon at this time were divided into three main classes. The ruling class of wealthy priests, merchants, landowners, and warriors was called the *awilu*. Below these were the more numerous *musheknu*, which consisted of merchants, artisans, and those who served the royal court. Finally there were the *wardu*, slaves. Babylonian society relied on slavery for workers in agriculture and trade. Slaves were classed as lifetime slaves, those who had, for example, been captured during wars, and short-term slaves, people who became slaves for a defined period either as a punishment under law or because children were sold by their parents as slaves for an agreed period. Notably, Hammurabi's Code of Laws applied to all three levels of Babylonian society.

In 1755 BCE, Babylon was the single most important and powerful city in the world, and it was difficult to see how anyone could challenge it. What we now know is that the success of Hammurabi and the growing power of Babylon contained the seeds of its destruction.

Chapter Three

Hittite, Kassite, and Assyrian Rule

"The young king, though unproven when he took the throne, would go on to show himself as an able general and ruler."

—Duncan Ryan, referring to Hittite King Mursili

There is no doubt that Hammurabi was efficient and effective both as an administrator and as a military leader. However, he was also what we would now call a micro manager—he was unwilling to delegate any of his functions as king and he tended to personally oversee everything from construction projects to the conduct of battles. In the short term, this ensured success, but it also meant that Hammurabi failed to put in place a bureaucratic infrastructure of civil servants and subsidiary military leaders. This wasn't a problem as long as the king was energetic and able, but it meant that the rise and power of Babylon were directly associated with the personality of Hammurabi. This was a dangerous situation for any nation-state.

By 1750 BCE, Hammurabi was around 60 years of age and had become increasingly frail. In this year he passed the rule of Babylon to his son, Samsu-iluna. Hammurabi died later the same year. There is no evidence that Samsu-iluna or any of the subsequent rulers of Babylon were inefficient or inattentive, but it also clear that none had the administrative genius or energy of Hammurabi, and in the next 150 years Babylon gradually declined in importance and power.

The first areas of Babylonia to revolt were the lands in the north, in what had previously been Assyrian territory. These lands conquered by Hammurabi returned to control of the Assyrians within twenty years of his death. In the south of Mesopotamia, a group of provinces and cities known collectively as Sealand revolted against Babylonian rule and established their own independent kingdom where they reverted to Akkadian (rather than Amorite) language and culture. Confusingly this kingdom is sometimes known as the Second Dynasty of Babylon even though it had nothing to do with the Amorite-ruled city of Babylon.

Later, the resurgent Elamites were able to take back their territory in eastern Mesopotamia, and by the seventeenth century BCE, Babylon was simply one of many city-states in Mesopotamia. At the same time that the power of Babylon was declining, a new empire was rising in the north. The Hittites were an Anatolian people centered in the city of Hattusa near the Kızılırmak River in what is now Turkey. Around 1595 BCE, under the control of a new king, Mursili I, the Hittites began to move south, into Mesopotamia in a campaign against the Amorites.

Hittite armies swept down the Euphrates River and conquered the weakened Babylon in 1595 BCE. King Mursili seems to have considered incorporating Babylon into the expanding Hittite Empire but concluded that it was simply too far from their homelands to be effectively defended. Instead the city was ransacked and destroyed, and the last Amorite ruler of Babylon, Samsu-Ditana, was overthrown. Internal disputes regarding the leadership of the Hittite people combined with an attack from the Hurrians from the east of Anatolia meant that the Hittites were then forced to withdraw to their homeland quickly.

Babylon was handed over to allies of the Hittites, the Kassites, a warlike tribe from the Zagros Mountains of northwestern Iran. The Kassites ruled Babylon for over 400 years, and during that time they removed almost every trace of Amorite rule from the city. During this period, Babylon even lost its name, becoming Karduniash. Unlike its previous rulers, the Kassites do not seem to have been interested in art or science, and they left very little writing which has led to the early period of their rule being called the Dark Age of Babylon. It appears that the Kassites put in place their own king and established a new ruling class, mainly military leaders, who took effective control of the city, though they were careful to allow the inhabitants of the city to continue to worship the same gods as they had under Amorite rule. Kassite control extended to other former Amorite cities in the area including Larsa, Sippar, Nippur, and Susa. Under the Kassites, Babylon became once again one of the most important trading centers in Mesopotamia even as it declined in importance as a scientific and cultural center.

The Kassites were trapped between two powerful and growing empires. The Assyrian Empire to the north of Babylon had recovered from the defeats inflicted on it by Hammurabi and was becoming the most powerful state in the region. The Empire of Elam in the east of Mesopotamia was also growing in influence. Rather than seeking to confront their powerful neighbors with military force, the Kassites instead chose to establish alliances with both the Assyrian and Elamite Empires. These alliances were reinforced by intermarriage between the ruling families of Babylon and its two neighboring empires, and this cautious diplomacy ensured that Babylon was left in peace for a time to grow prosperous once more.

Inevitably, as Babylon became wealthier, both the Elamites and the Assyrians began to consider ways of increasing their influence in the city. In 1365 BCE, a new king took the throne of the Assyrian Empire, Ashur-uballit I. It quickly became obvious that this new king was ambitious; he defeated King Shuttarna II of the Hurri-Mitanni Empire, giving Assyria control over the northern part of Mesopotamia. The Kassite king of Babylon, Burna-Buriash II, (or according to some scholars his son and successor Kara-ḫardaš) married the Assyrian king's daughter, which further strengthened ties between Babylon and the rapidly growing Assyrian Empire. However, not everyone in Babylon was happy with this move—some of the Kassite ruling families were concerned about what they saw as undue and growing Assyrian influence in the city. They reacted by murdering Kara-ḥardaš and installing their own man, Nazi-Bugaš, as king of Babylon.

Ashur-uballit reacted swiftly, attacking and conquering the city and having Nazi-Bugaš and the conspirators executed. In 1332 BCE, a new Kassite king of Babylon, Kurigalzu II, was installed by Ashur-uballit. Nominally, Babylon remained an independent city ruled by the Kassites, but the installation of a new king by the Assyrians made it clear that the city would continue to exist only while it enjoyed the approval of the Assyrian king.

During the following one hundred years, the Kassites together with the Hittites and the Mitanni attempted to slow the relentless expansion of the Assyrian Empire. Despite their efforts, Kashtiliash IV would become the last Kassite king to rule Babylon in around 1235 BCE. The Assyrians were at this time fully committed to a war with the Hittites, and King Kashtiliash IV seems to have taken advantage of this distraction to occupy and fortify lands between Babylon and Assyria. This was a fatal mistake. The Assyrian king, Tukulti-Ninurta, attacked and sacked Babylon, destroying many buildings, stealing the treasures from its temples and taking many of its citizens (including King Kashtiliash) back to Assyria as prisoners and slaves. To prevent any further rebellions, the Assyrians finally also installed their own ruler, Enlil-nadin-shumi, on the throne in Babylon, who served as a viceroy to Tukulti-Ninurta.

From this time on, the Assyrians in the north and Elamites in the east continued to encroach on the Kassites' Babylonian territories, annexing lands seemingly at will until in 1155 BCE when the Kassites were finally completely overthrown by Shutruk-Nakhunte of Elam. The Elamites, who at this point were at war with the Assyrians, could not hold on to Babylon for long, giving room for a new Akkadian-speaking south Mesopotamian dynasty to place a king upon the Babylonian throne. With the coronation of Marduk-kabit-ahheshu, the Fourth Dynasty of Babylon from Isin, also known as the Second Dynasty of Isin, was founded. Marduk-kabit-ahheshu was only the second native Mesopotamian to rule Babylon.

Although the dynasty managed to stay in power for around 125 years and enjoyed some successes (namely Nebuchadnezzar I's defeat of the Elamites in the late twelfth century BCE), these new Akkadian-speaking kings proved incapable to stand up to the Assyrian Empire in the long run. Weakened by conflicts with the powerful Assyrians and a terrible famine, Babylon was eventually was swamped by waves of settlers from the deserts of the Levant including Arameans, Suteans, and Chaldeans. These new groups made little attempt to assimilate into the existing Babylonian society and instead took control of parts of the city for themselves and formed their own political power blocks. There were a number of kings throughout the next 300 years, coming from a range of ethnic and racial backgrounds—these years are often referred to as the Second Dark Age because of the chaotic nature of the period and the lack of written sources. The

Kassites even made a short comeback when they regained control over Babylon around the turn of the millennium.

By 900 BCE, the Assyrians were once again on the rise, and the Neo-Assyrian Empire had become the most powerful in the world. Assyrian troops were highly trained, their commanders were tactically astute, and their armies were provided with iron weapons and armor, making them virtually invincible on the battlefield. Babylon became little more than a footnote in the history of the Neo-Assyrian Empire.

Chapter Four

The Destruction and Rebuilding of Babylon

"The Assyrian came down like the wolf on the fold,
And his cohorts were gleaming in purple and gold."

—Lord Byron, The Destruction of Sennacherib

In 722 BCE, a new king came to the throne in Assyria. Sargon II would prove to be a great leader, a very able military tactician, and a prolific builder of temples, public buildings, and even cities. He would also found the Sargonid Dynasty which would rule the Neo-Assyrian Empire for the next one hundred years. Under Sargon II's rule, Assyria conquered Samaria and destroyed the kingdom of Israel.

In 721 BCE, Sargon received news that a local tribal chieftain, Marduk-Baladan, had declared himself king of Babylon. Marduk-Baladan allied Babylon with the Elamites, and it was clear that he was preparing to mount a challenge to Assyrian control of the city.

Sargon marched south with his army and met the combined forces of Elam and Babylon near the city of Der in 720 BCE. The Assyrian forces were routed, and Babylon briefly remained an independent city. For the next few years, Sargon built up his military forces in a series of successful campaigns against the kingdom of Urartu. In 710 BCE, Sargon returned to Babylon, and this time, he made no mistakes. He devastated the smaller towns and villages in the area and then attacked, conquered, and sacked the city. Marduk-Baladan fled south and, surprisingly, Sargon chose not to pursue him.

Sargon installed himself as king of Babylon, and for the next three years, he lived in the royal palace where he entertained envoys from many of the most powerful kings in the region. When Sargon II was killed in battle in 705 BCE, he was succeeded by his son, Sennacherib. Sennacherib based himself in the Assyrian capital of Nineveh and did not bother to visit Babylon—he simply sent a message pointing out that he was now the king. Incensed by this perceived slight, the people of Babylon welcomed back Marduk-Baladan who once again installed himself as king of Babylon in 703 BCE. Even then, Sennacherib did not bother to go to Babylon. Instead he sent one of his military commanders with orders to eject Marduk-Baladan. Instead, the combined forces of the Elamites, Babylonians, and Aramaeans defeated the Assyrian army in a battle in 703 BCE.

Angered by the outcome, Sennacherib reacted by leading the Assyrian army himself against Babylon, and this time, he defeated the Babylonians and Elamites. Marduk-Baladan managed to escape capture once again, but nonetheless, Sennacherib was free to install a new king in Babylon. His choice was Bel-ibni, but he proved to be so inept that he was eventually replaced by Ashur-nadin-shumi, Sennacherib's son and heir. His rule would not be long-lived, and around 694 BCE, Ashur-nadin-shumi was kidnapped and murdered by the Elamites who installed their own king in Babylon. This provoked a full-scale war between Elam and Assyria which raged for four years, devastating swaths of Mesopotamia. The Assyrians were unable to completely defeat the Elamites, and Sennacherib retired to Nineveh; for a few years there was peace. But the Assyrian king did not forget about the role of Babylon in the murder of his favorite son and heir.

In 689 BCE, the Elamite king died, and Sennacherib took advantage of the ensuing disputes about who should replace him to march south to attack Babylon once again. This time, he was determined to teach the Babylonians a lesson that the world would never forget. Without the support of the distracted Elamites, the Babylonian armies were quickly defeated. We know from a cuneiform tablet what Sennacherib did next:

"I swiftly marched to Babylon which I was intent upon conquering. I blew like the onrush of a hurricane and enveloped the city like a fog. I completely surrounded it and captured it by breaching and scaling the walls. I did not spare his mighty warriors, young or old, but filled the city square with their corpses. . . . The city and houses I completely destroyed from foundations to roof and set fire to them. I tore down both inner and outer city walls, temples, temple-towers made of brick and clay—as many as there were—and threw everything into the Arahtu canal. I dug a ditch inside the city and thereby levelled off the earth on its site with water. I destroyed even the outline of its foundations. I flattened it more than any flood could have done. In order that the site of that city and its temples would never be remembered, I devastated it with water so that it became a mere meadow."

The city of Babylon, repository of wealth and knowledge for more than a thousand years was not just destroyed—it was obliterated. Even the mighty statue of Marduk, the principal god of Babylon, was taken from the city square and removed to Nineveh as a reminder of the wrath of Sennacherib. However, this desecration of Marduk would prove to be the undoing of Sennacherib. The Assyrians and Babylonians worshipped many of the same gods, and Marduk, the god who brought order out of chaos, was one of the most revered. Many Assyrians were horrified at this insult to an important god, and in 681 BCE, Sennacherib was assassinated by his own eldest sons, possibly as an act of atonement for this insult to the gods.

Following the killing of Sennacherib, there was a brief civil war in Assyria between Esarhaddon, Sennacherib's youngest son, and his two older brothers who had carried out the murder. In just six weeks of fighting, Esarhaddon defeated his elder brothers, and in the spring of 681 BCE, he was crowned king of Assyria. His brothers fled into exile, and their families and supporters were executed. One of Esarhaddon's first acts as king was to announce that the devastated city of Babylon would be rebuilt, and the religious statues and other artifacts removed by Sennacherib would be returned. The rebuilding of the city progressed quickly, and as soon as the Esagila, the temple to Marduk, was complete, the giant statue of the god was returned from Nineveh to its rightful place. Esarhaddon was also careful not to offend the people of Babylon by taking the title of king of the city and ensuring that he spent part of each year in his rebuilt palace within the city. Before Esarhaddon died in 669 BCE, he named his eldest son, Shamash-shum-ukin, as the new king of Babylon and his younger son, Ashurbanipal, as king of Assyria.

It didn't take long for the two sons to begin to compete with one another. Shamash-shum-ukin allied with the Elamites, Persians, and other local tribes against his brother and the Assyrian Empire. After a series of battles, Shamash-shum-ukin was defeated and killed, and Ashurbanipal installed a loyal Assyrian, Kandalanu, as the new king of Babylon. When Ashurbanipal died in 627 BCE, the Assyrian Empire was undermined by a series of wars of succession and its control over Babylon weakened. Babylon, like many other cities in the region, took advantage of the increasing weakness of the Assyrians to make a bid for independence.

Chapter Five

The Neo-Babylonian Empire

"While such is its size, in magnificence there is no other city that approaches to it."

—Herodotus

In 620 BCE, a new king took the throne in Babylon. Nabopolassar was the chief of a Chaldean tribe, and he would remain king in Babylon for almost twenty years. Sensing a shift in the balance of power in the region, Nabopolassar formed alliances with Cyaxares, king of the Medes and Persians, and with both the Cimmerians and the Scythians. Within ten years of taking the throne, Nabopolassar had united most of Mesopotamia under Babylonian control. Then, he turned his attention to the Assyrians and their Egyptian allies.

By 612 BCE, a combined army of Babylon and the Medes attacked the Assyrian capital city of Nineveh. Following a long siege, the city fell later that year, signaling not just freedom for Babylon but the end of the once mighty Assyrian Empire. Nabopolassar also successfully fought the Egyptians and, by the time of his death in 605 BCE, Babylon was once again the capital of a large empire.

Nabopolassar was succeeded by his son, Nebuchadnezzar II, who set out to restore the city of Babylon to its former glory. He built new temples and ziggurats, restored and improved existing buildings, and extended and rebuilt the city walls to incorporate towers and fortifications. He had a wide bridge constructed over the Euphrates River to connect the old and new parts of the city and is even said to have opened a museum (perhaps the first in the world) in one of the royal palace complexes. He also enlarged the Temple of Marduk and created a broad, processional way through the city, leading from this temple to the lavishly decorated Ishtar Gate in the inner city walls. Each spring equinox, a great festival would be held in which the statue of the god Marduk would be carried from the temple in the center of the city out through the Ishtar Gate to a temple outside the city walls. Then, with great ceremony, it would be returned.

The city of Babylon became famous throughout Mesopotamia for the magnificence of its private and public buildings. Herodotus, the Greek writer and historian who has been called the "Father of History" described Babylon after its restoration in his *Histories*.

"The city stands on a broad plain, and is an exact square, a hundred and twenty stadia (twenty-three kilometers) in length each way, so that the entire circuit is four hundred and eighty stadia. While such is its size, in magnificence there is no other city that approaches to it. It is surrounded, in the first place, by a broad and deep moat, full of water, behind which rises a wall fifty royal cubits in width and two hundred (over one hundred meters) in height."

However, the most famous feature of the city, which became identified by the Greeks as one of the seven wonders of the ancient world, were said to be its hanging gardens. These gardens were first mentioned by a Babylonian priest, Berossus, in 290 BCE, but the earliest surviving detailed description was provided by the first-century BCE Greek historian Diodorus Siculus in his mammoth book *Bibliotheca historica* (Universal History). He tells in this book of a square garden, 120 meters to a side, built on a series of raised platforms which elevated it above the level of the city walls. The garden was built as a series of ascending terraces which "sloped like a hillside and the several parts of the structure rose from one another tier on tier, the appearance of the whole resembled that of a theatre." The gardens were planted with large trees as well as flora from Iran and Persia and broad paths and avenues wound throughout. Several royal apartments were constructed in the gardens, and irrigation was done by "machines for supplying the garden with water, the machines raising the water in great abundance from the river, although no one outside could see it being done."

The gardens were said to have been constructed on the orders of Nebuchadnezzar II for his Iranian wife, Queen Amytis, because she missed the green, rolling landscape of her homeland. The gardens were built next to a magnificent palace created for the new king which was modestly called "The Marvel of Mankind." However, modern archeologists and historians have cast doubts on whether the fabled hanging gardens ever really existed at all. No trace of them has been found during extensive excavations of the ancient city of Babylon and, though contemporary writings mention many of Nebuchadnezzar's construction projects, none specifically mention a magnificent garden. Some historians consider that later historians such as Diodorus Siculus have mistakenly described a garden which was actually built by Assyrian King Sennacherib in his capital city, Nineveh.

Even if we can't be certain that the hanging gardens existed, we do know that Nebuchadnezzar's Babylon was a mighty and magnificent city. Even now, the archeological site which covers the remains of this city is over 2,000 acres in size, making it the largest archeological site in the Middle East. Contemporary writings suggest that the citizens of Babylon at this time considered the city to be an earthly version of paradise, a symbol of the unity that the god Marduk had brought in place of the chaos that had gone before. No other ancient city was as revered, discussed, and feared as Babylon under the rule of Nebuchadnezzar.

For more than forty years, Nebuchadnezzar ruled from this mighty city an empire which stretched from the mountains of Anatolia to parts of Egypt. His conquests included Jerusalem after which he exiled the Jews from their homeland, forcing them to live in Babylonian territories. When he died in 562 BCE and passed the throne to his son, Amel-Marduk, it seemed that the Neo-Babylonian Empire was set to dominate Mesopotamia for a very long time indeed.

Amel-Marduk, however, reigned for only two years before being murdered and succeeded by Neriglissar, Nebuchadnezzar II's son-in-law. Neriglissar died young, and his son and successor, who was still only a boy, would not fare any better when he was killed in 556 BCE after only a few months on the throne.

Although the next king managed to stay in power longer than his predecessors, he proved to be much less popular. Nabonidus was a follower of the cult of the moon god, Sin, and he attempted to suppress the worship of Marduk, which made him very unpopular with the influential priesthood and the mass of the Babylonian people. He also alienated his army leaders by showing no interest in military affairs and delegating these to his young son, Belshazzar. These issues caused dissent and fragmentation within the Neo-Babylonian Empire, and when it was required to face a new external threat, it proved too weak to do so.

Because of this, the Neo-Babylonian Empire lasted less than 25 years after the death of Nebuchadnezzar II.

Chapter Six

The Persian Conquest

"Marduk, the great lord, established as his fate for me a magnanimous heart of one who loves Babylon, and I daily attended to his worship."

—Cyrus the Great

Pars Province is one of the thirty-one provinces of Iran. In around 559 BCE, a new king inherited the throne of the city of Anshan. This king, Cyrus, would go on to become one of the most powerful leaders in the ancient world and would expand his small kingdom into the largest the world had seen at that time. Cyrus began by extending his rule over all of Pars Province so that he began to call himself king of Persia (Persia was an alternative name by which Pars was known).

This angered the Medes who controlled northwestern Iran and parts of Mesopotamia. Astyages, the king of the Medes, decided to curb the ambitions of the new king and launched an attack on Persia in 550 BCE. The resulting war lasted for three years and resulted in the complete defeat of the Median Empire. However, Cyrus proved to be as astute in victory as he had proved as a military leader. Instead of having the defeated king executed, he spared his life and married Astyages' daughter, Amytis.

This pacified the Median nobles who might otherwise have opposed Persian rule; many nobles were also incorporated by Cyrus into a new administration. In addition, Cyrus was careful not to offend the religious sensibilities of those people he had conquered, allowing them to continue to worship in the same way. This was, for the period, an enlightened approach which made rebellion in conquered provinces less likely.

After Cyrus overthrew the Median kingdom, he turned his attention to the Lydian Empire in western Anatolia under the rule of King Croesus. By 540 BCE, Cyrus, who was by now known as "Cyrus the Great," had completely defeated the Lydians. King Croesus was not only allowed to live, but he also became an important advisor in Cyrus' court. During this period the Persians also captured several territories from the Greeks, but there was one more empire in the immediate area that represented a challenge to the growing Persian Empire— the Neo-Babylonian Empire. Babylon was at this point still weakened by internal disagreement following the death of Nebuchadnezzar II.

In 539 BCE, Cyrus the Great began his attack on the Babylonians. First, he captured the kingdom of Elam with very little difficulty. Then his armies moved down the Tigris River towards Babylon itself. Later that year, the armies of Babylon and Persia finally met in battle near the important town of Opis, north of Babylon. The battle resulted in a complete rout of all Babylonian forces, and two days later, the Persians arrived outside the walls of the city itself.

It is said that when Cyrus saw the mighty walls of the city, he realized that it would not be possible to take the city by force. Instead, during a Babylonian religious ceremony, Persian troops partially diverted the Euphrates River upstream of the city. The sudden drop in the water level allowed Persian troops to wade across and enter the city through openings in the walls which were normally underwater. The city was taken almost without a fight.

Cyrus proved to be wise in his treatment of the captured city. He denounced the unpopular King Nabonidus because of his suppression of the worship of the god Marduk and, under the Persian occupation, many temples to Marduk were refurbished and rebuilt, as were cult sanctuaries dedicated to Marduk. After the conquest of Babylon and all the lands it had formerly controlled, Cyrus declared himself to be "King of Babylon, king of Sumer and Akkad, king of the four corners of the world." He also released all the Jews who had been exiled by Nebuchadnezzar and allowed them to return to Jerusalem and to rebuild their temples.

Babylon would remain part of the growing Achaemenid Empire for the next 200 years. It became the capital of the Ninth Satrap of the Empire and its administrative center. Under Persian rule, science and art flourished in the city once more, and Babylonian astronomers made a number of significant discoveries and produced some of the first maps of the constellations. It has been said that that the Greek philosopher Thales of Miletus (now regarded as the first western philosopher) may have studied in Babylon during this period and that

Pythagoras developed his theorem based on previous work by Babylonian mathematicians. The city of Babylon enjoyed peace and wealth under Persian control. But, as the Persian Empire began to weaken, things rapidly deteriorated.

By the time that Persian King Darius III came to rule the Achaemenid Empire in 336 BCE, it was substantially weaker than it had been under Cyrus. Many of the satraps which comprised the provinces of the empire had become rebellious, partly because of cripplingly high taxes imposed by the central government to pay for continuing wars. Babylon's temples, streets, and canals began to fall into disrepair. There were even attempts at rebellion against the Persians—Babylonian kings were briefly able to claim the throne, but were unable to retain it in the face of Persian military might.

Meanwhile a young man had assumed the throne in the far distant kingdom of Macedon in Greece. No-one could guess that this man, in what remained of his short life, would become the most powerful and successful military leader that the world had ever seen, or that his empire would eclipse all those that had come before.

Chapter Seven

Alexander the Great Enters Babylon

"His genius was such that he ended an epoch and began another—but one of unceasing war and misery."

—Ernst Badian

In the summer of 336 BCE, Philip II, king of the Greek province of Macedon, was assassinated. His twenty-year-old son Alexander was immediately proclaimed king. Alexander quickly consolidated his position by having a number of potential rivals executed. The death of King Philip had encouraged several Greek states to rebel, but these were promptly and efficiently dealt with by Alexander who was declared *Hegemon* (leader) of all Greek forces.

In 334 BCE, Alexander led his army of over 50,000 troops across the Hellespont. As he set foot on Asian soil for the first time, Alexander hurled his spear into the ground, announcing that he was happy to accept Asia as a gift from the gods. From the very start it was clear that this charismatic young leader had ambitions that stretched well beyond Greece.

Throughout 334 BCE, the armies of Alexander and the Persian armies under the command of Darius III clashed in a series of battles. In each, the Persians were defeated and Alexander's troops occupied more territory. In the following year, Alexander occupied Syria and the Levant and inflicted such a decisive defeat on the Persians at the Battle of Issus that Darius III was forced to flee from the battlefield, leaving his army to be annihilated. In 332 BCE, Alexander continued his seemingly inexorable string of conquests by taking Egypt and founding the city of Alexandria. Then, in 331 BCE, he turned his attention to Mesopotamia and in particular towards Persian-controlled Babylon.

Darius understood that losing Mesopotamia and Babylon, the administrative center of his empire, would be a disaster, and he spent the period following his defeat at Issus in Babylon, improving and enlarging his armies. By the time that Alexander began his move towards Mesopotamia, Darius had accumulated a vast army— Greek historian Diodorus Siculus claimed that Darius forces numbered more than two-hundred thousand cavalry and more than one million infantry supported by scythed chariots and war elephants. Modern historians doubt that the army was quite this large, but the Persian army which awaited Alexander in Mesopotamia was probably the largest military force ever to take the field at this time.

Facing this was Alexander's army of forty thousand infantry supported by seven thousand cavalry. On paper at least, it didn't seem that the young Greek leader stood a chance. Darius left Babylon with his army and marched to Gaugamela, east of Mosul in modern-day northern Iraq. The Persians took up position and awaited the arrival of the Greeks. Alexander took his armies across the Euphrates and the Tigris Rivers and arrived at the battlefield at Gaugamela towards the end of 331 BCE.

The battle which followed was brief, brutal, and bloody and demonstrated Alexander's complete mastery of the art of war. By careful tactical maneuvering, his smaller army was able to defeat the much larger Persian forces. The Persian army fled the field, leaving behind its chariots, war elephants, and a vast treasure. Darius fled once again, but he was quickly assassinated by his own general and cousin Bessus and with him died the Achaemenid Empire. Nothing now stood between Alexander and Babylon.

Alexander marched south and occupied Babylon without a fight. He had already made it clear that he had a great fondness for the city, and he ordered his soldiers not to loot it or to harm the inhabitants or enter their homes. Contemporary sources suggest that Alexander may have planned to make Babylon the capital of his new empire and a center of learning and the arts. He even ordered that the great ziggurat in the center of the city, which had been allowed to become rather dilapidated, should be torn down so that it could be rebuilt and made even more splendid.

However, Alexander did not spend much time in Babylon. He had himself crowned king of Babylon and then set off to conquer what remained of the Persian

Empire. This was quickly achieved, and Alexander next turned his attention to India. But, having conquered a large part of that country, Alexander's weary and depleted army finally rebelled and refused to cross the River Ganges. In 324 BCE, Alexander arrived back in Mesopotamia to find that many of the local governors he had left in charge had failed to carry out his instructions. He promptly had them executed.

At around this time Alexander's second-in-command, friend, and possibly lover, Hephaestion, died either from illness or due to poisoning. Alexander was inconsolable. He had Hephaestion's doctor executed and ordered that the whole of his now vast empire went through a period of official mourning. By 323 BCE, he had returned to live in the city of Babylon and his drinking, which had always been legendary, grew even worse. In June, he entertained his admiral Nearchus and his friend Medius of Larissa at his palace in Babylon. All attendees drank a great deal, and afterward Alexander fell ill. Within a couple of weeks, he was dead, aged just 32.

Historians have speculated on the cause of his death; possible explanations include malaria, an infection caused by drinking dirty water, meningitis, or even poisoning. Whatever the actual cause, the most powerful military leader in the world was suddenly dead, and his demise left a power vacuum which would tear his empire apart. While ill, he had been asked who should inherit his role as leader. His only answer, "the strongest," virtually ensured conflict and violence to decide who his replacement should be.

Alexander's generals, Cassander, Ptolemy, Antigonus, and Seleucus (who became known as part of the *Diadochi*—"successors") fought over control of his empire for the next forty years. Seleucus, who founded the Seleucid Empire, which included Mesopotamia, Anatolia, and parts of India, lasted longer than any of the others and became King Seleucus I Nicator ("the Conqueror"). However, Seleucus did not share Alexander's reverence for the city of Babylon, and none of the improvements that Alexander had planned for the city were ever completed.

During the fighting amongst the Diadochi, the population gradually drifted away from the city of Babylon. In 275 BCE, it appears that those who remained were transported to Seleucia, and the city was left virtually abandoned.

Chapter Eight

Babylon Falls

"Babylon is fallen, is fallen! And all the carved images of her gods He has broken to the ground."

—Isaiah 21:9

Babylon never seems to have recovered from the deportation of its people in the period following Alexander's death. Occupants did filter gradually back into the city, but it never became the thriving metropolis it had once been. Seleucid rule in Mesopotamia was replaced by the Parthian Empire from Iran under the rule of King Mithridates around 144 BCE. By 116 CE, Roman forces under the command of Emperor Trajan briefly took control of the area, after which the Parthians reclaimed control. This, in turn, was replaced by the control of the Sasanian Empire from Persia in 226 CE. However, during this period Babylonia was no more than a series of settlements and was regarded only as a province of relatively minor importance by those who controlled it. The city itself fell into disrepair, and blocks and bricks from temples and the once mighty walls were taken to build dwellings.

In the first and second centuries CE, Christianity arrived in Babylon. The Church of the East originated in the Sasanian Empire as part of Syriac Christianity, and its influence spread across the lands controlled by the empire. A bishop of the Church of the East was established in Babylon and remained there for many hundreds of years.

During the seventh century CE, the Sasanian Empire was gradually conquered by Arab Muslims. In 638 CE, Mesopotamia was under Muslim rule, and Christianity became marginalized in those regions. By the mid-seventh century, Babylonia ceased to exist as an independent province and was subsumed into the Rashidun Caliphate under the rule of Caliph Uthman.

In the tenth century AD, the Muslim writer, traveler, and geographer Muhammad Abu'l-Qasim Ibn Hawqal completed his most famous work, *The Face of the Earth*, which provided a detailed description of the lands ruled by the Rashidun Caliphate. The only mention of Babylon occurs when it is noted that the writer visited "a small village called Babel" in the land that was once known as Mesopotamia. Subsequent travelers who wrote about this area mention only ruins gradually being covered by the desert sands.

By the medieval period, contemporary Muslim writings noted the ruins of Babylon only as a source of bricks which were used in construction projects in Baghdad and Basra—a tragic end for a city that was once the mightiest in the world.

The ruins of Babylon lay undiscovered and disregarded until European archeologists began to search for the remains of the city in the seventeenth century.

Initially there was confusion about the location of the ruins (some people thought that the city of Baghdad had been built on the same location as Babylon). The Italian writer and traveler Pietro della Valle is generally credited with the modern re-discovery of Babylon in the early seventeenth century.

By the 1800s, historians and archeologists from Europe were making regular trips to this area. British historian and writer Claudius James Rich described in his *Memoir on the Ruins of Babylon* (1815) what he had found while excavating the site: "Instead of a few insulated mounds, I found the whole face of the country covered with vestiges of building, in some places consisting of brick walls surprisingly fresh, in others merely of a vast succession of mounds of rubbish of such indeterminate figures, variety and extent, as to involve the person who should have formed any theory in inextricable confusion."

The ruins of Babylon were frequently excavated during the twentieth century and became an important cultural asset and tourist destination for Iraq. Sadly, a great deal of damage was caused to the site during the American-led invasion of Iraq in 2003 when units of the First Marine Expeditionary Force used the site to build a military camp, leveling large areas to make room for a helipad and a parking area for military vehicles and causing extensive damage to the remains of the Ishtar Gate.

The remains of Babylon re-opened to the public in 2009, but the difficult and dangerous political situation in Iraq has meant that few people have visited, and those that do are disappointed to see that an oil pipeline now runs through part of the site.

Chapter Nine

Babylon in the Bible

"Babylon the great, mother of prostitutes and of earth's abominations."

—Revelations

One of the reasons that Babylon became of such surpassing interest to European historians and archeologists is its association with the Bible. Babylon is mentioned more than almost any other Mesopotamian city in the Bible and is often used as the personification of greed, wealth, and godlessness. In Genesis, the founding of Babel (Babylon) is described and credited to a king named Nimrod, a descendant of Noah's son Ham. Genesis also notes that, after the Great Flood, the survivors all spoke a single language and worshipped a single god.

Genesis describes the building of a great tower in the city of Babel which was so high that its "top may reach unto heaven." However, the magnificence of the city and the staggering size of the tower encouraged the inhabitants of Babel to become arrogant, and in order to punish them, God scattered the people of Babel across the Earth and condemned them to use many different languages so that they were no longer able to understand one another.

Early European archeologists hoped that they might find the remains of the tower of Babel in the ruins of Babylon. They were disappointed. There certainly was a large ziggurat in the center of Babylon which was believed to have been between two and three hundred feet tall. This was the Etemenanki, the "temple of the foundation of heaven and earth" and part of a temple complex dedicated to the god Marduk. It seems very likely this was the original of the Tower of Babel from the Bible. It is now known that Alexander the Great had the Etemenanki torn down with the intention of having it completely rebuilt. However, he died before this could be done and his successors showed no interest in this project. It is very likely that the bricks which had formed the Tower of Babel were appropriated instead by locals for their own building projects, and all that archeologists have been able to discover is a small, swampy area of land in the ruins of Babylon which may have been the site of the base of the ziggurat.

The books of the Old Testament frequently mention Babylon, and in particular the destruction of Jerusalem and the exile of the Jews to Babylon. King Nebuchadnezzar II is specifically mentioned in the Bible, though he is described as a wicked tyrant who stole sacred items from the Jewish Temple in Jerusalem. When his "son" Belshazzar (Belshazzar was in reality the regent and son of the last Neo-Babylonian king, Nabonidus) took the throne, the Bible describes in the Book of Daniel how he holds a feast at which the objects stolen from the Jews are used. Those attending are then terrified when a ghostly hand appears and writes a mysterious message on the wall. Daniel, who is in exile in Babylon, is brought in to decipher the message and tells the king: "God has numbered the days of your reign . . . Your kingdom is divided and given to the Medes and Persians." The story is a description of the fall of Babylon in 539 BCE when Babylon was conquered by the Persian king, Cyrus the Great.

Babylon is also mentioned in the New Testament, notably in the Revelation of St. John where the city is symbolized as the "Whore of Babylon," which is a female figure riding on a scarlet beast with seven heads and ten horns. Written on her head are the words: "Babylon the great, mother of prostitutes and of earth's abominations." In the Christian Bible, Babylon is used as a symbol of those who reject the Word of God and who are obsessed with the material world. In Isaiah there is a final mention of the city: "Babylon is fallen, is fallen! And all the carved images of her gods He has broken to the ground."

It isn't just the Christian Bible that Babylon is given prominence. In the Hebrew Bible, Babylon is mentioned many times, mainly in relation to the destruction of Jerusalem and the exile of the Jews. In the Hebrew Bible, Babylon is synonymous with the oppression of the righteous and the imposition of a foreign religion. In the Rastafarian belief system, the name of Babylon is used to symbolize a world obsessed by material possessions and in particular is used to denote the United States of America because Jamaicans were brought there as slaves in the same way that Jews were taken to Babylon. Even in

Freemasonry, which has its own versions of Biblical accounts, Babylon is mentioned, claiming that the city is the birthplace of Freemasonry and the source of much scientific and occult knowledge.

Even in modern culture, the name of this city survives when the names of most of its contemporaries are unknown to anyone but historical scholars. When Warner Bros. commissioned a science-fiction space opera for television based on a giant space station designed for inter-planetary and inter-species trade, they called the space station (and the show) *Babylon 5*. A science-fiction action movie released in 2008 and set in a future, dystopian New York City was given the title *Babylon A.D.*

Even though it has been more than two thousand years since Babylon was a powerful and influential city, its name lives on in the modern world.

Conclusion

Although Babylon is often referred to as if it was a single entity, the truth is that there were many Babylons, each quite different in terms of beliefs and their place in the ancient world. Babylon first came briefly to prominence under the rule of King Hammurabi in the eighteenth century BCE. During the forty years of his rule, Babylon became the largest city in the world, a center of learning and the arts, and the heart of a large empire. However, with Hammurabi's death, the city rapidly declined to become just one more city-state in Mesopotamia.

It wasn't until more than one thousand years had passed that Nebuchadnezzar II would come to the throne and once again make Babylon the ruler of an empire and a revered center for science and learning. Much of what we think we know about the city of Babylon dates from this period, though it seems even famous things like the Hanging Gardens may not actually have existed. It's certainly true that the city became wealthy during this period and famous for the magnificence of its temples and other buildings. However, the Neo-Babylonian Empire barely survived the death of Nebuchadnezzar, and within twenty-five years it had been conquered by the Persians.

Although it remained a significant city for another five hundred years, surviving occupation by the forces of Alexander the Great, Babylon never regained its power or prestige. The fact that Alexander planned to make Babylon the capital of his vast empire might have restored

Introduction

The very word Babylon is resonant with images of prosperity, magnificent buildings, and perhaps also with arrogance, decadence, and the worship of wealth and material possessions. But what was the reality of this ancient city which is still remembered today long after most of its contemporaries have been forgotten?

Babylon had a history more convoluted and more turbulent than most great cities. In a period of around two thousand years, it went from being a small city-state amongst many to the magnificent heart of an empire revered for its learning and culture. Then it declined, was destroyed and re-built, and eventually became the heart of an even larger empire. When Alexander the Great conquered a large part of the civilized world, he chose Babylon to be the capital of his mighty empire, and it seemed that the city was destined for immortality.

Instead, Alexander died mysteriously in the city which then fell into decline once again and within a few hundred years had become little more than a series of ruins in the desert, providing a useful source of bricks for local builders. This is the story of the rise and fall of the most famous of all the ancient cities of Mesopotamia. This is the story of Babylon.

Chapter One

First Babylonian Dynasty

"If history, as by most definitions, begins with writing, then the birth, rise and fall of ancient Mesopotamia occupies a full half of all history."

—Paul Kriwaczek

The fertile land between the Tigris and Euphrates Rivers, the area known as Mesopotamia, was the cradle of human civilization. The Sumerians settled this area in around 3000 BCE, bringing with them irrigation and new, more efficient methods of farming. They also introduced technologies such as the wheel and the ability to smelt bronze which transformed the societies in this part of the world. The Sumerians also introduced writing, enabling them to pass on their knowledge and beliefs.

The Sumerians lived in a series of city-states, semi-autonomous and fortified towns ruled by kings and each with their own laws and religious beliefs. Then, around 2300 BCE, the Sumerians were challenged by the leader of Akkad, a Semitic-speaking city-state to the north. The ruler of this city, Sargon of Akkad (also known as Sargon the Great), sought to extend the power of Akkad by conquering the Sumer city-states. After defeating the Sumer army close to the Sumer city of Uruk in the biggest it once again to fame and glory, but the young Macedonian king died before he could begin rebuilding the city.

After that, Babylon declined rapidly until, six hundred years later, it was little more than a village in the desert. Two hundred years after that, it was no more than a source of bricks for local building projects. When it was mighty, Babylon was the most influential and powerful city in the world. After its fall, Babylon rapidly became nothing but a memory.

Made in the USA
Las Vegas, NV
20 August 2022

53658848R00030